Zodiac Embroidery

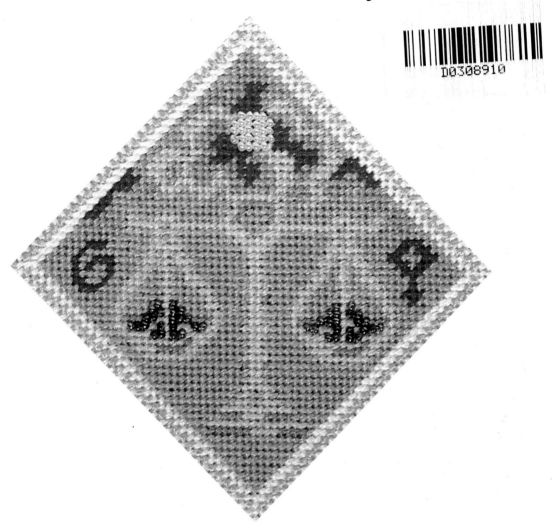

For Stuart

Zodiac Embroidery

Sylvia Drinkwater

SEARCH PRESS

First published in Great Britain 1991
Search Press Limited,
Wellwood, North Farm Road,
Tunbridge Wells, Kent TN2 3DR

Photographs by Search Press Studio

ISBN 085532 656 5

The author wishes to thank the many friends who encouraged
her with this book and the following embroiderers and artists for
their help:–

Cancer footstool embroidered by Lila Burridge

Libra embroidered by Joan Roberts

Taurus shoulder-bag embroidered by Iris Hughes

Virgo evening purse, Capricorn, alphabets and numbers
embroidered by Dorn Woodiwiss

Alphabets designed to match the embroideries and drawn by
Frank Foster

Gemini embroidered by Enid Goldby

Composition by Genesis Typesetting, Rochester, Kent

Printed and bound by Times Publishing Group, Singapore.

Contents

Introduction

The twelve signs of the Zodiac are represented by extremely visual and colourful motifs and even within each individual sign, they offer endless scope for design and usage. Canvas work is the perfect medium for capturing the subtleties of the outlines and colouring of each sign and further interest can be added by applying beads or embroidery stitches to the finished design.

These twelve signs are divided into the four elements of our planet, being governed either by air, earth, fire or water. The colours used to work each sign should therefore reflect these characteristics, ranging from the soft, moody blues and greens of water for Pisces, to the blazing reds and yellows of fire for Leo.

Each sign is also govened by one, or more, ruling planets, including the sun and the moon. We are all believed to be influenced by these planets and they affect our temperament and our character, depending on our date and time of birth. A special astrological symbol represents each planet and a stylized motif is also used to depict individual signs, such as a lion's head for Leo, the curled horns of the ram for Aries and a scorpion for Scorpio, the sign with the sting in it stail!

Whether you take these beliefs seriously or not is a matter of personal choice but all of these motifs and symbols are interesting and make suitable designs for the craft of canvas work. To incorporate all the elements of each sign, the main characteristics on most of the designs are shown as a central diamond motif, surrounded by four corner designs which are loosely based on the appropriate Zodiac symbol, planetary sign, and the flower and number traditionally linked with that sign. For example, Aries is shown in the central diamond

as a ram; the top left-hand corner shows the horn symbol; the top right-hand corner the number nine; the bottom left-hand corner the honeysuckle and the bottom right-hand corner, the planetary symbol.

For the beginner who wishes to explore the craft of canvas work the book gives details of the type of canvas and yarn available and hints on colour combining to achieve subtle effects. It also gives instructions on how to prepare an embroidery frame to hold the canvas, and the stitches used. It then goes on to explain how to read the charts given for each sign and how to stretch and mount the completed picture. More experienced embroiderers will be interested in the instructions for working miniature designs on silk gauze.

It must be pointed out that for the purposes of photography, most of the designs have been mounted and then framed, or incorporated into another article, so that you cannot always see the full extent of the canvas. However, the corresponding chart for each sign does illustrate the full size of the canvas, including all the lettering. In case you wish to add your own personal message, or your signature and the date to complete an embroidery, you can use the alphabets, together with the figures shown on page 62.

When completed these embroideries can be used in many different ways. Worked as miniatures and suitably mounted they would make delightfully personal greetings cards. On a larger scale they can be used for attractive chair seats, wall hangings, cushions, bags or even to embellish clothing.

The craft of canvas work

How to begin

Canvas work is simply embroidery on canvas and although many stitches are suitable for this medium, most people prefer to use tent stitch. The stitches must cover the entire surface of the material and the finished work presents a woven appearance almost akin to tapestry. This probably explains why canvas work is sometimes erroneously described as 'tapestry'. Once a canvas has been completed it can be further embellished by adding areas of embroidery, such as cross stitch and French knots, to give it surface texture.

This craft has a practical as well as a decorative purpose and it reached the height of its glory during the late seventeenth and early eighteenth centuries. During the nineteenth century it deteriorated into the poor designs and gaudy colouring of Berlin woolwork, so popular in Victorian days. It was rescued from this unhappy state by the William Morris movement and takes its place today among the most prestigious forms of embroidery.

The basic tools and materials required are minimal and inexpensive – just canvas, needles, thread and a suitable embroidery frame. This section gives details of the canvas and thread available, how to work the simple stitches and gives useful information on colour combining. It goes on to explain how to read an embroidery chart and the final stages of stretching and mounting the completed canvas.

Canvas

Canvas is made of a single thread or double thread mesh and the mesh sizes are governed by the number of vertical (warp) threads to 2.5cm (1in). It can be made from linen, hemp, flax, silk or gauze. Mono, or single thread canvas is better for work in tent stitch and the

fig 1

single thread canvas

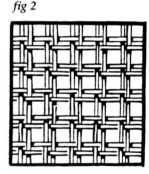

fig 2

double thread canvas

mesh count varies from as many as 24 to as few as 3 threads to 2.5cm (1in), see Fig 1.

Double thread canvas is woven as pairs of threads and is suitable for cross stitch and other more solid stitches, see Fig 2. Stitches can be worked over the pairs of thread or it can be converted into a single canvas by pressing the threads apart with a needle so that they are evenly distributed. This is referred to as 'pricking the canvas' and is a useful tip for working finer effects. In figure embroidery the hands and face can be worked in tent stitch, while the costume and background remain in cross stitch.

It is always advisable to use the best quality canvas available. A linen canvas with a lock on the horizontal (weft) threads will not distort when it is embroidered and will retain its shape when in use. All of the designs in this book have been worked on single canvas but you may wish to adapt them for other purposes.

Yarn

Always buy a good quality yarn suitable for the type of canvas being used. It must be thick enough to cover the canvas completely but fine enough to pull easily through the holes. The golden rule is to select a wool, silk or cotton yarn bearing a proportional relationship to the canvas background.

Traditionally, tapestry and crewel wools are used in canvas work as they are hard-wearing and colourfast. Crewel wool is thinner than tapestry wool but it may be used as a double thickness. For smaller articles, single silk or mercerised threads are used and silk can be mixed with wool to produce a greater effect of light and shade. Six-stranded mercerised cotton has been used for all of the designs in this book, with the exception of the miniatures.

If wool, in particular, is threaded into the needle the wrong way, or against the grain, it will become roughened and may break during stitching. To find the right way, stroke it between your fingers and you will feel it has a 'rough' and a 'smooth' surface. Thread the smooth end into the needle and cut into lengths of no more than 45cm (18in), or it will wear thin.

Do not begin with a knot but run the end in and out of the canvas and then cover with the embroidery. Finish off in the same way at the back of the work by running the yarn under the threads. When working a design in many different colours, it helps to bring the colour being dropped to the front of the work, then remove the needle and leave it until it is required again. This obviates the necessity of continually finishing off and keeps the back of the canvas tidy. It is generally better to begin at the bottom left-hand corner and work upwards but it is quite in order to begin at the top if you

prefer. In either case the completed embroidery should be covered with a cloth when you leave it for any length of time.

Colour combining

All of the designs in this book are worked without outlines in small, solid areas of colour, as you would see in nature. The colours of the threads chosen to work the embroideries therefore need a noticeable contrast, one from the other, to stop them merging together. For example, the design for Cancer uses five greens which, although in the same colour family, must be different enough for each to show clearly when they are placed side by side.

The design for Scorpio was originally worked on a small piece of canvas and had another panel added to enable the name to be embroidered under the symbols. Although skilfully executed, this slight change in the dye lot of the colour can be detected. This also applies to the design for the Leo embroidery. It is therefore necessary to emphasize the importance of buying sufficient thread of the same dye lot to enable you to complete the canvas. Sufficient quantities have been estimated to allow for areas of the embroidery to be unpicked, if necessary, but not for any additional lettering you may wish to add.

Needles

Tapestry needles which are blunt-ended with a large eye are used for canvas work. They are sold in a variety of sizes but should be large enough to thread comfortably and small enough to pass easily through the holes, otherwise you will distort the canvas.

The largest is size 13 and this is suitable for working on rug canvas. The smallest is size 26 and this is fine enough to work a miniature on silk gauze. You can also use crewel needles on fine silk gauze.

Frames

Canvas work can be held in the hand and worked but it is easier, and quicker, to work on a canvas which has been stretched over a frame. This helps keep the stitches at an even tension and the threads are easier to count, also the design can be seen as a whole.

Home-made frame

A simple frame can be made very cheaply from four pieces of wood, cut to form a true rectangle or square, see Fig 3.

The canvas can be fixed to the frame with staples or pinned with thumb tacks to the front of the frame, working from the centre of each side outwards.

Ready-made frame

Ready-made, or slate frames, are usually rectangular and can be used for all types of embroidery. They consist of a long rail at the top and the bottom with strips of webbing attached, and stetcher bars at each side which slot into the ends of the rails. These are held in place with adjustable pegs or screws, see Fig 4.

Ring frame or embroidery hoop

A ring frame may be used for working miniatures on silk gauze or an even-weave fabric but should *never* be used for canvas, as the pressure distorts the mesh.

The frame consists of one wooden ring fitted inside another between which the fabric is held in place and stretched, with the fabric surface uppermost. Lay the fabric, right side up, over the inner ring and press the outer ring over it. Gently ease the fabric out, keeping the grain straight, and tighten the screw to secure, see Fig 5.

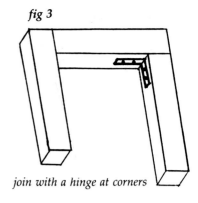

fig 3

join with a hinge at corners

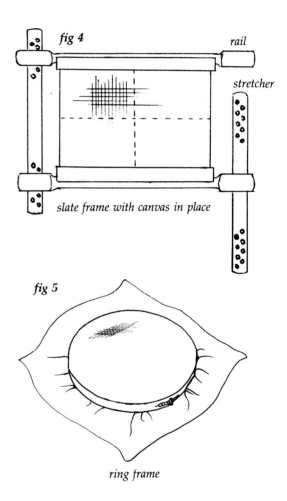

fig 4 rail

stretcher

slate frame with canvas in place

fig 5

ring frame

Preparing the canvas

Cut the canvas *at least* 7.5 to 10cm (3 to 4in) larger than the size of the finished design. This allows for the final blocking and mounting of the canvas.

Before putting the canvas into the frame, it helps to bind the raw edges with masking tape to prevent them fraying.

Framing the canvas

On a home-made frame the whole canvas should be attached to the front of the frame with staples or thumb-tacks.

Make sure the grain of the canvas is straight and fix it to the frame in the centre of each side. Now continue fixing the canvas from the centre outwards, see Fig 6.

On a slate frame, attach the top and bottom edges of the canvas to the rails but first mark the centre of the canvas and each rail. If the edges of the canvas have not been bound, turn them in and stitch them down to secure them. Match the centre marks and overcast the canvas to both strips of webbing, working from the centre outwards, see Fig 7. Insert the stretchers, adjust their position until the canvas is taut, then secure them with pegs. With strong thread, lace the side edges of the canvas to the stretchers and tie the thread firmly to secure, see Fig 8.

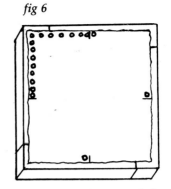

fig 6

fabric on the front of home-made frame

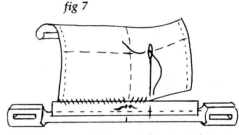

fig 7

overcast canvas to the webbing on slate frame

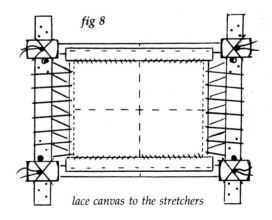

fig 8

lace canvas to the stretchers

11

Embroidery stitches

The designs featured in this book are worked in tent stitch, with the addition of an occasional cross stitch, back stitch or French knot. By using a frame with a stand, or by propping one end of a frame without a stand on a table with the other end in your lap, both hands are left free for stitching. Using one hand below the canvas to push the needle up and the other hand above to catch it and send it down again speeds up the work and produces a smoother, more even surface.

Tent stitch

This stitch is worked from lower left to upper right across one complete intersection of the canvas. You can also work the stitch from the left-hand lower hole to the right-hand top hole across the canvas, see Fig 9, or from the right-hand top hole to the left-hand lower hole, see Fig 10, but the stitches must always lie in the same direction.

Try, where possible, to bring the needle 'up' through an empty hole and 'down' again through the hole with a stitch already worked into it, as bringing the needle up into the stitch can split the thread. Keeping the needle straight, make each stitch in two movements. Each stitch will sit correctly on the canvas when the thread is worked in the correct direction from stitch to stitch.

It is either shown as a coloured square, or an open square, on the charts given in this book.

Back stitch

This is worked over the tent stitch and one thread of the canvas in any dirction. Bring the needle through from the back to the front, take it back across the canvas and down again into the next hole. Carry the needle across the back of the canvas and bring it through to the front again one hole in front of the previous stitch, and continue in this way.

Back stitch is shown as a small diagonal line on the charts given in this book, for example, see the mouth and nostrils of Aries.

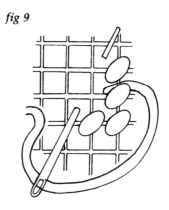

fig 9

tent stitch worked left to right

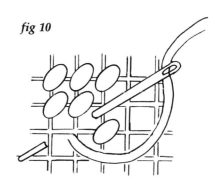

fig 10

tent stitch worked right to left

Cross stitch

The first half of a cross stitch is formed by the existing tent stitch and the second half crosses over the first, to form the completed stitch. The second half of the stitch must always go in the same direction, from lower right to upper left.

Cross stitch is shown as a cross on the charts given in this book, for example, see the eyes of Aries.

This little Victorian footstool shows another use for a completed canvas.
The sign shown here is for Cancer.
Embroidered by Lila Burridge.

French knot

To work a French knot, bring the threaded needle through the canvas to the front at the position required. Hold the thread taut round the needle with the thumb, see Fig 11, by twisting the needle round the thread and turning the needle completely round in a clockwise direction.

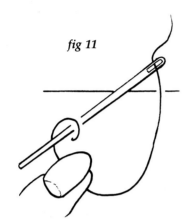

fig 11

hold thread taut to begin a French knot

Put the point of the needle back through the canvas to the right of where it came up. Press the thumb on the thread to keep it taut until it is completely drawn through to the back of the work, see Fig 12. Don't pull too tightly but just leave the knot sitting on top of the tent stitches.

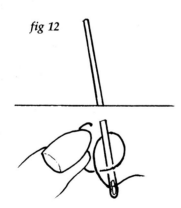

fig 12

hold thread taut to pull it through to the back

A French knot is shown as a dot on the charts given in this book, for example, see the eye of each fish of Pisces.

Reading the charts

Each square on the chart represents a stitch in a particular colour and is the equivalent of an intersection of two threads on the canvas. Always count the threads on the canvas and not the holes, see Fig 13. When the squares are coloured in, or left blank, it indicates that a tent stitch is to be worked. For the other symbols used, see Fig 14.

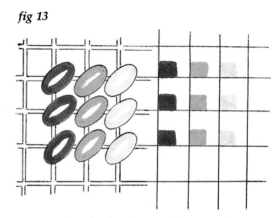

fig 13

counting the threads to work tent stitch

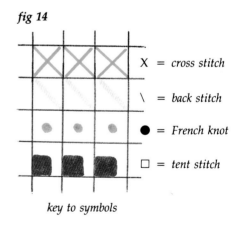

fig 14

X = cross stitch

\ = back stitch

● = French knot

□ = tent stitch

key to symbols

14

In some instances, you may prefer to colour in the background before beginning to embroider. Most craft or art shops will be able to supply you with a suitable fabric paint which is fast drying. In this example, see Fig 15, the background is painted blue to stop the white canvas showing through the dark thread. Do always test the colour first on a scrap of canvas and always allow the paint to dry thoroughly before beginning to embroider.

fig 15   *painted background*

Order of working the colours

Where possible embroider the lighter colours first, then progressively fill in with the darker colours. If the darker colours are worked first, they will show through where they are carried across the back of the canvas.

Begin each design with the white diamond outline, matching the points along the canvas thread. When the whole diamond motif is completed, work the corners with the white outline first, then the wording and, lastly, the background. If a darker colour needs to be carried across the back of bare canvas, catch it over the back of some of the stitches already worked in an adjacent area.

While stitching, the yarn may become twisted. If so, just dangle the needle on the thread and it will unravel itself automatically.

Size of picture

Using a larger, or smaller mesh canvas will either increase or reduce the size of the finished picture. For example, a design worked on 14 threads of 2.5cm (1in) canvas measuring 15 × 20cm (6 × 8in) will increase in size to approximately 21.5 × 28cm (8½ × 11in) if worked on a canvas with 10 threads to 2.5cm (1in).

You will also need to increase or reduce the number of strands of mercerised cotton threads being used. If working on a larger mesh use 8 or 9 strands instead of 6 to cover the canvas. If working on a smaller mesh, use 3 or 4 strands instead of 6. You will need to experiment to arrive at the number of threads needed to cover the canvas completely.

On larger mesh canvas, tapestry wool would be a suitable alternative or two strands of crewel wool.

How to complete a canvas

When an embroidery is completed the canvas will have to be stretched and then it can either be mounted and framed, or made into a wall hanging or incorporated into another item, such as a bag. Before you take the canvas out of the frame, think about signing and dating your work.

A picture, well framed behind glass, should last for a hundred years or more, provided it is protected from dust, damp and too much light. Many textiles in the past have deteriorated because of the poor quality of the materials used for mounting and framing. Most art shops will undertake this for you but if you prefer to complete the whole project yourself, you can obtain the necessary materials from the same source.

Obviously, an unprotected embroidery, such as a wall hanging will not last as long as a framed picture and where the canvas is incorporated into an item which will be used on an everyday basis, wear-and-tear will eventually take its toll.

Stretching

Canvas should never be ironed but must be stretched into shape. Pressing will only flatten the stitches and without proper stretching, the canvas will not be correctly 'squared' up. Before you begin to stretch the canvas, first spray the back of the embroidery with clear water.

Cover a drawing board, which must be larger than the finished size of the picture, with layers of slightly dampened absorbent paper – plain kitchen towels would be ideal. Now pin lengths of string horizontally and vertically across the board, outlining the required finished size of the picture. Place the canvas face downwards on the paper, within the marked lines. Working from the centre and using rustless thumb tacks, pin the top edge firmly to the board, parallel with the edge of the board and stretching where necessary to extend the canvas to the outlined size required. Begin again in the centre of each side and, finally, the lower edge, pinning and stretching into shape, see Fig 1. Check the measurements and make sure that the sides are at right angles. Allow to dry naturally, when the canvas will harden again.

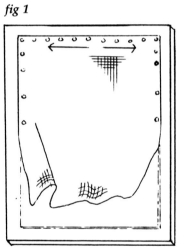

fig 1

stretching canvas into shape

Mounting

If you are going to frame a picture it must first be mounted. Use a piece of hardboard rather than cardboard which may contain harmful acids and absorb damp. Cut this slightly smaller than the required finished size of the picture. Lay this piece of board on the back of the embroidery and, beginning at the top, fold the fabric over to the back and pin the canvas to

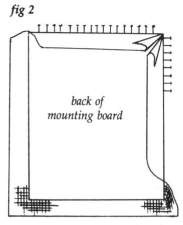

fig 2

back of mounting board

mounting canvas on board, back view

the edge of the board, see Fig 2. Fold the canvas to the back along the side and lower edges and continue pinning in the same way. Keep checking that the front of the canvas is positioned correctly and add more pins where necessary.

The canvas can now be laced in position across the back of the board. With a long length of strong thread, begin at the centre and work outwards, lacing the canvas vertically from the top to the lower edge, pulling the thread firmly and continually checking that the picture has not moved. Now work horizontal rows of lacing in the same way, weaving the thread through the vertical strands, see Fig 3. Cut and neaten the corners, removing any excess bulk

and fasten off the thread securely. If required, the back of the picture can now be neatened by stitching on a hemmed piece of fine cotton fabric.

Framing

The components that go to make up the complete frame will include the picture frame itself, the glass, a suitable backing board and your stretched and mounted canvas, see Fig 4. Old frames are very attractive and can sometimes be picked up very cheaply at jumble sales but the backing material will probably need replacing. Make sure that the frame you intend to use has a moulding which is deep enough to take the mounted canvas and the thickness of the hardboard backing.

Before assembling the picture make sure that the frame and glass are clean, then place the mounted canvas face downwards on the inside of the glass and frame. Pin the backing board in place with panel pins, lightly tapped into the inner edges of the frame. Attach picture hooks and a cord, or picture wire if the frame is heavy.

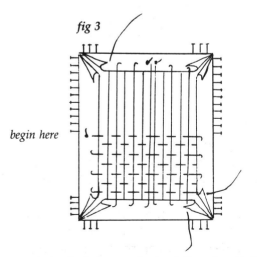

fig 3

begin here

lacing back of canvas horizontally and vertically

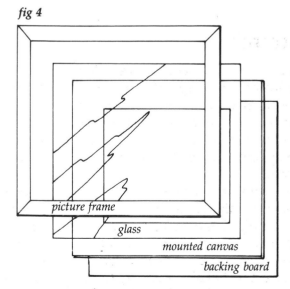

fig 4

picture frame

glass

mounted canvas

backing board

frame components

Miniature embroideries

Each of the miniatures featured in this book is worked entirely in tent stitch, with the addition of an occasional back stitch or cross stitch, see page 12 for details. They are embroidered from the same charts as the larger designs and in the same colours.

When completed, these delicate examples of the craft of canvas work can be framed in the same way as the larger versions, see page 16 for details, applied to a bag or an item of clothing, or mounted as a greetings card. Details are given here for mounting a greetings card to mark a special birthday anniversary.

Materials

A small piece of silk gauze, which can be bought to size

Note: The zodiac designs vary in size, so work out the amount of gauze needed as follows: count the number of stitches on the chosen zodiac chart both vertically and horizontally. Allow for a border all round to give the final size required, noting that this border has been masked in the illustrations shown here. As an example, the chart for Aries has 95 stitches across and 124 stitches down, plus a border of 30 stitches all round, so will require a piece of gauze measuring 155 by 184 threads. Depending on the mesh size, usually 30 to 2.5cm (1in), the size of gauze needed would be approximately 13.5 × 16cm (5¼ × 6¼in)

Calico to fit into a ring frame

One spool of machine silk in each colour required

Crewel needle size 8, noting that size 26 tapestry needle may not be small enough

Ring frame

Magnifying glass, if required

Instructions

Machine the square of silk gauze to the centre of the calico. Before beginning to embroider, cut out the calico from behind the silk gauze square, close to the stitching, otherwise you will be stitching through the calico as well. Stretch the calico into a ring embroidery frame, see Fig 1.

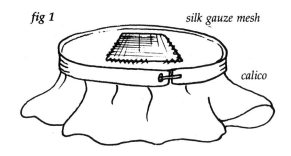

fig 1   silk gauze mesh

calico

The evening bag shown here has been quilted with the signs and symbols
of Virgo, then embellished with a miniature of the sign.
Embroidered by Dorn Woodiwiss.

fig 2

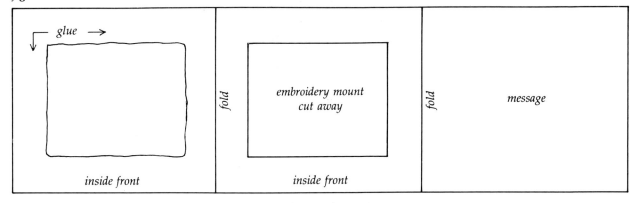

greetings card mount

How to mount a greetings card

A wide selection of pre-cut mounts is available from most art shops, complete with matching envelopes, and these will give your miniature embroidery a professional finish. It is a simple matter, however, to make your own mounts to any size and the card, or paper you use will vary in price according to the quality and weight. Choose the colour of your mount very carefully, making sure it will enhance your embroidery. Before finally deciding on the size and colour of your mount, make sure you can obtain a suitable envelope to match.

Cutting the mount

In addition to the mounting card you will also need sharp scissors, a ruler for trimming the card to size and some glue. Rubber solution is recommended, as it allows the embroidery to be repositioned if necessary.

Cut a rectangle from the card and fold this into three, making sure that this size will accommodate the embroidery. The left-hand side should be 3mm (⅛in) smaller than the other two sections to avoid catching in the fold. In the middle section, which will be the inside of the front of the card, mark an area large enough to allow a full view of the design, allowing about 1cm (½in) of the embroidery to be stuck down all round, and leaving a margin of at least 2.5cm (1in) all round the edges of the card. Cut out this area, see Fig 2.

With the right side of the embroidery facing you, lightly apply the glue to the extreme edges, as directed. Place the embroidery face down on to the inside of the cut-out opening, making sure it is correctly positioned.

Once the glue is dry, fold the left-hand side over the back of the embroidery and glue down, then fold the card in half so that the embroidery shows on the front and write your message on the inside.

The signs of
the Zodiac

The signs of the Zodiac

The following dates given for each sign may differ slightly from one astrologer to another and people born on, or near the change from one sign to the next, referred to as the 'cusp', may exhibit characteristics of either, or both of the two neighbouring signs. As well as giving each sign its individual character, the planets which govern them are classifed as positive (or masculine), and negative (or feminine). Each sign also comes under one of the four elements, air, earth, fire and water and is described as a cardinal, fixed or mutable sign.

The astrological year begins with Aries, represented by the ram, covering the period from about the 21st March to the 20th April. Its characteristics are fire, positive and cardinal. The signs then continue in the following order. Taurus, the bull, 21st April to the 20th May; earth, negative, fixed. Gemini, the twins, 21st May to the 21st June; air, positive, mutable. Cancer, the crab, 22nd June to the 22nd July; water, negative, cardinal. Leo, the lion, 23rd July to the 22nd August; fire, positive, fixed. Virgo, the virgin, 23rd August to the 22nd September; earth, negative, mutable. Libra, the scales, 23rd September to the 22nd October; air, positive, cardinal. Scorpio, the scorpion, 23rd October to the 22nd November; water, negative, fixed. Sagittarius, the archer, 23rd November to the 22nd December; fire, positive, mutable. Capricorn, the goat, 23rd December to the 20th January; earth, negative, cardinal. Aquarius, the water carrier, 21st January to the 19th February; air, positive, fixed. Pisces, the fishes, 20th February to the 20th March; water, negative, mutable.

Positive signs are spontaneous and expressive, while negative signs tend to the withdrawn and passive. The elements also affect character, so that air signs have a lively attitude; earth signs are controlled and matter-of-fact; fire signs shine but can be aggressive, while water signs are sensitive and intuitive. The cardinal element indicates initiative, the fixed element steadfastness and the mutable sign is changeable and adaptable.

The zodiac has always been associated with magic and, where possible, this aspect has been introduced into the following designs, by using the 'magic square' of the chessboard. This is formed by linking the 'fixed' moves of the knight around the chessboard and the resulting pattern, see below, is the basis of the corner designs on some of the embroideries.

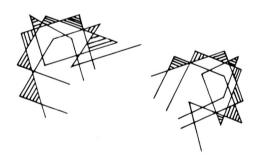

These diagrams illustrate how a magic square is formed.

Aries

21st March to 20th April
Aries is usually a leader and has a positive
and forceful personality, in fact,
the action sign of the zodiac.

Materials

Single canvas of 14 to 16 threads to 2.5cm (1in),
measuring 28 × 33cm (11 × 13in)
Blunt-ended needle size 18
6-stranded mercerised cotton skeins in 12
colours, as follows:-
2 skeins white
1 skein yellow (fleece, face and corners)
1 skein gold (fleece, tail and corners)
2 skeins orange (fleece and corners)
2 skeins bright red (symbols, horns, fleece and
lettering)
1 skein dark red (fleece, horns and corner)
1 skein wine (horn shadows, feet and features)
1 skein leaf-green (leaves)
3 skeins bright turquoise (background of
diamond and leaves)
1 skein dark turquoise (corners)
1 skein, or few threads of pink (honeysuckle)
8 skeins dark Prussian blue (background)

Instructions

Tent stitch is used throughout, except for the
following:-
1) Cross stitch in wine for the eyes and in dark
red in the topknot.
2) Back stitch in wine for the left nostril and left
side of mouth, worked over the white tent
stitches with 6 threads.
See page 24 for chart.

To complete

There is a full alphabet for Aries, see page 64
for chart.
The finished picture measures approximately
17 × 23cm (6¾ × 9in).

First sign of the zodiac
A fire sign
Positive
Cardinal
Ruling planet, Mars
Motif, the ram
Colours, all bright hues of red
Gemstones, bloodstone and aquamarine

Metal, iron
Flowers, honeysuckle and geranium
Plants, garlic and cayenne
Flavour, pungent
Tree, thorn
Day, Tuesday
Number, 9
Keyword, pioneer

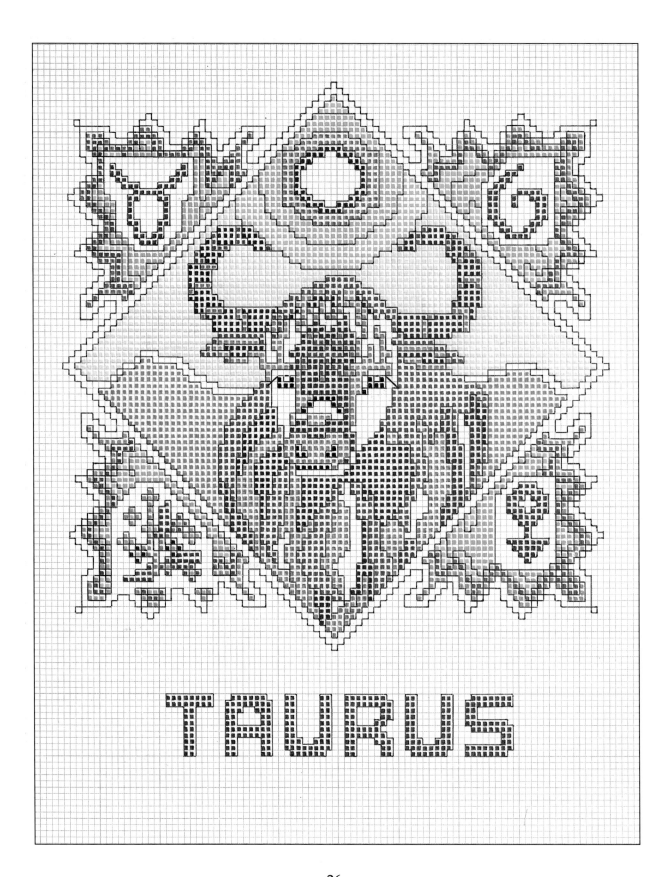

Taurus

21st April to 20th May
Taurus likes domestic harmony,
to be surrounded by beautiful things
and is creative in a practical way.

Materials

Single canvas of 14 to 16 threads to 2.5cm (1in), measuring 30 × 35cm (11¾ × 13¾in)
Blunt-ended needle size 18
6-stranded mercerised cotton skeins in 14 colours, as follows:-
2 skeins white
1 skein bright yellow (forget-me-nots)
1 skein emerald green (corners and lettering)
1 skein pale pink (muzzle and corners)
2 skeins rose pink (hide, horns and corners)
1 skein pale green (background of diamond and corners)
6 skeins Prussian blue (background)
1 skein indigo (eyes, nostrils and mouth)
1 skein French navy (hide, horns and first halo)
1 skein royal blue (hide, nose and body)
1 skein medium blue (hide and second halo)
2 skeins delphinium blue (third halo and corners)
2 skeins pale blue (fourth halo and corners)
2 skeins ice blue (background of diamond)

Instructions

Tent stitch is used throughout, except for the following:-
1) The eylashes are in straight stitch in indigo, worked over the tent stitch as shown on the chart.
2) On the forget-me-nots the petals can be left in tent stitch, or worked in cross stitch.
See page 26 for chart.

To complete

There is a full alphabet for Taurus, see page 63 for chart.
The finished picture measures approximately 20 × 24cm (7¾ × 9½in).

Second sign of the zodiac
An earth sign
Negative
Fixed
Ruling planet, Venus
Motif, the bull
Colours, deep blue, sky blue, deep rose, emerald and pale green
Gemstones, emerald, diamond and sapphire

Metal, copper
Flowers, forget-me-not and rose
Plants, sage and thyme
Flavour, sweet
Tree, apple
Day, Friday
Number, 6
Keyword, opulent

Gemini

21st May to 21st June
The intellectual characteristics of Gemini make them good teachers.
They like to investigate mysteries and they are practical
with their hands.

Materials

Single canvas of 16 to 16 threads to 2.5cm (1in), measuring 26 × 35cm (10¼ × 13¾in)
Blunt-ended needle size 18
6-stranded mercerised cotton skeins in 12 colours, as follows:-
1 skein pale yellow (blouse)
1 skein pale orange (blouse)
1 skein deep gold (hair)
2 skeins pale gold (hair)
1 skein flesh
2 skeins dark turquoise (background of diamond and lettering)
2 skeins pale turquoise (background of diamond and lettering)
6 skeins beige (shown as open squares on background, see illustration)
7 skeins white (shown as open squares on background, see illustration)
1 skein pale brown
1 skein, or two lengths, dark brown
1 skein silver grey cotton perlé (used double)

The alternative illustrated embroidery is worked in wool on 10 threads to 2.5cm (1in) canvas. It is designed so that it can be fitted around a tubular lampshade frame, with the hair and fingers of the twins touching on both sides, noting that the side edging in turquoise is omitted. It measures approximately 35.5 × 23cm (14 × 9in).

Instructions

Tent stitch is used throughout, except for the following:-
1) The faces and right cuffs outlined in 2 strands of pale brown in back stitch.
2) Left cuff outlined in 2 strands of dark brown in back stitch.
3) Lower right and upper left sides of the diamonds worked in dark turquoise in back stitch over the tent stitch.
See page 30 for chart.

Third sign of the zodiac
An air sign
Positive
Mutable
Ruling planet, Mercury
Motif, the twins
Colours, yellow, orange, grey, azure blue and light blue
Gemstones, emerald, lapis lazuli and opal

Metal, quicksilver
Flowers, lily of the valley and flax
Plants, parsley and caraway
Flavour, astringent
Tree, chestnut
Day, Wednesday
Number, 5
Keyword, conversation

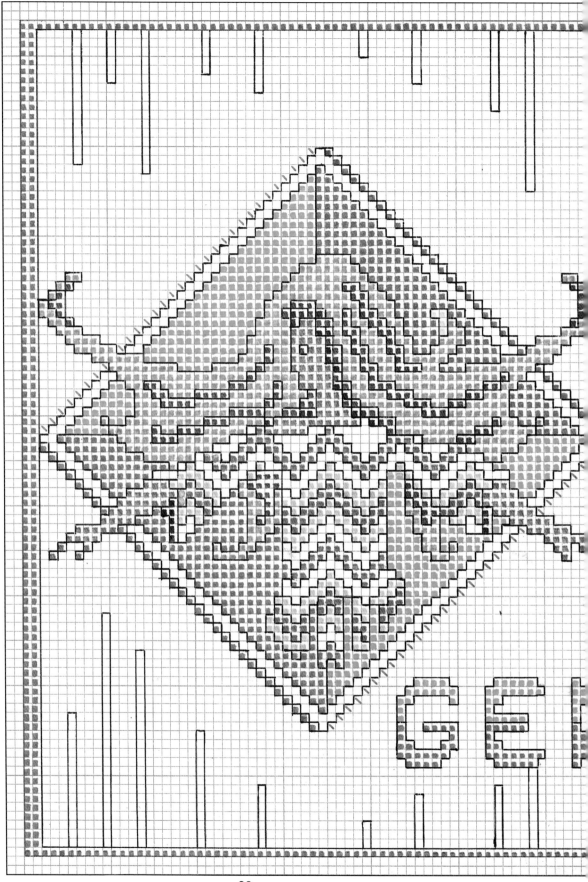

The symbols for Gemini, shown on the separate chart, can be added to the embroidery. Place them horizontally above and opposite the word 'Gemini' and work them in the same colours.

To position them on the embroidery, count the number of stitches between the diamond points, both across and down, to make sure they are central. The symbols measure 48 stitches across and 10 stitches down. This means that they should be placed 4 stitches above and 9 stitches in from the top diamond stitch in white.

To complete

There is a full alphabet for Gemini, see page 63 for chart.

The finished picture measures approximately 16.5 × 25.5cm (6½ × 10in).

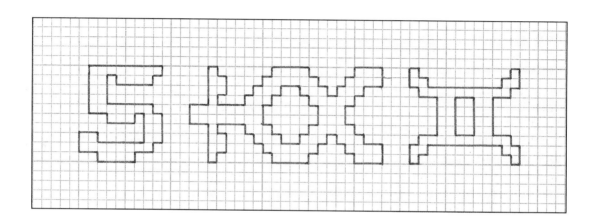

Cancer

22nd June to 22nd July
Cancer is a conscientious and creative worker,
also the perfect homemaker. This sign likes to feel
proud of their achievements.

Materials

Single canvas of 14 to 16 threads to 2.5cm (1in), measuring 30 × 33cm (11¾ × 13in)
Blunt-ended needle size 18
6-stranded mercerised cotton skeins in 10 colours, as follows:-
2 skeins white
3 skeins dark blue (claws, sea edge and lettering)
3 skeins delphinium blue (claws, sea edge and lettering)
7 skeins ice-blue (background)
1 skein bottle green (claws and leaves)
2 skeins bright emerald green (shell)
1 skein lighter emerald green (claws, leaves and shell decoration)
2 skeins apple green (sea edge and lettering)
1 skein light olive green (shell and claws)
7 skeins sea-green (central background)

Instructions

Tent stitch is used throughout, except for the following:-
1) The two white eyes are worked in cross stitch.
See page 36 for chart.

To complete

There is a full embroidered alphabet for Cancer, see page 62 for chart.
The finished picture measures approximately 22 × 24cm (8¾ × 9½in). The embroidery illustrated is worked on 15 threads to 2.5cm (1in) canvas.

Fourth sign of the zodiac
A water sign
Negative
Cardinal
Ruling planet, Moon
Motif, the crab
Colours, white, sea-green and ice-blue
Gemstones, pearl, emerald and aquamarine

Metal, silver
Flowers, magnolia and water lily
Plant, lettuce
Flavour, odourless
Tree, rubber
Day, Monday
Number, 2
Keyword, constant

Leo

23rd July to 22nd August
Leo likes a beautiful home and uses romantic self-expression
to achieve this. They are the artists of the zodiac.

Materials

Single canvas of 14 to 16 threads to 2.5cm (1in), measuring 23 × 28cm (9 × 11in)
Blunt-ended needle size 18
6-stranded mercerised cotton skeins in 12 colours, as follows:-
1 skein bright red (symbols and mane)
1 skein gold (mane)
1 skein orange (mane, lettering and corners)
1 skein cream (ears and mane edges)
1 skein pale yellow (nose)
1 skein lion yellow (face)
1 skein brown (features)
1 skein bright gold (sunflower and corners)
2 skeins light blue (background of diamond and corners)
2 skeins dark turquoise (background of diamond and corners)
6 skeins dark blue (background)
2 skeins white

Instructions

Tent stitch is used throughout, except for the following:-
1) Flowers by the name Leo, which have back stitch worked in orange over the tent stitch. See page 38 for chart.

To complete

There is no alphabet to match Leo, as the size would be disproportionate for more wording than simply 'Leo'. The alphabet for Scorpio would suit the embroidery for any additional details to be worked, see page 64 for chart.
The finished picture measures approximately 13 × 18cm (5 × 7in).

Fifth sign of the zodiac
A fire sign
Positive
Fixed
Ruling planet, Sun
Motif, the lion
Colours, hot orange and bright golden yellow
Gemstones, ruby and diamond

Metal, gold
Flowers, sunflower and peony
Plant, marigold
Flavour, zesty
Tree, palm
Day, Sunday
Number, 1
Keyword, independent

Virgo

23rd August to 22nd September
Virgo is a perfectionist and will be skilled at fine detailed work.
This sign is especially good at working with a magnifying glass,
or microscope, and possesses perception and logic.
With these qualities an embroidered miniature
would be an eminently suitable project.

Materials

Single canvas of 14 to 16 threads to 2.5cm (1in),
measuring 25.5 × 28cm (10 × 11in)
Blunt-ended needle size 18
6-stranded mercerised cotton skeins in 13
colours, as follows:-
1 skein pale yellow (hair and sleeve)
1 skein bright yellow (hair)
1 skein light orange (hair)
1 skein bright orange (hair and symbols)
1 skein white
1 skein grey (world)
2 skeins dark royal blue (symbols, moon and
lettering)
1 skein royal blue (symbols and sky)
2 skeins delphinium blue (dress, symbols and
sky)
1 skein medium blue (dress, symbols and sky)
1 skein light blue (dress, symbols and sky)
1 skein light grey-blue (outer sky)
6 skeins soft yellow (background)

Instructions

Tent stitch is used throughout, except for the
following:-
1) Two centre stitches of morning glory in
right-hand corner are in cross stitch.
2) The tips of some heather bells are in cross
stitch.
3) Back stitch joins the leaves of the heather.
See page 42 for chart.

To complete

There is a full alphabet for Virgo, see page 64
for chart.
The finished picture measures approximately
15 × 16.5cm (6 × 6½in).

Sixth sign of the zodiac
An earth sign
Negative
Mutable
Ruling planet, Mercury
Motif, the virgin
Esoteric ruler, Moon
The virgin is always shown holding
a wheat- sheaf.
Colours, grey, azure blue, light blue,
white and all the yellows

Gemstones, onyx, peridot and moonstone
Metals, quicksilver and nickel
Flowers, ling heather and morning glory
Plant, marsh-mallow
Flavour, piquant
Tree, hazel
Day, Friday
Number, 5
Keyword, analyse

Libra

23rd September to 22nd October
Libra is aesthetically inclined with a love of beauty and symmetry.
This makes them talented artists and designers,
especially of clothes.

Materials

Single canvas of 14 to 16 threads to 2.5cm (1in), measuring 25.5 × 28cm (10 × 11in)
Blunt-ended needle size 18
6-stranded mercerised cotton skeins in 13 colours, as follows:-
4 skeins cream (background)
1 skein white
1 skein brassy yellow (scales)
1 skein gold (scales)
1 skein cerise
1 skein rose pink
1 skein pastel pink
2 skeins sky blue (background of diamond)
1 skein olive green (stems)
1 skein dark emerald green (leaves)
1 skein mid-green (inner leaves and outer symbols)
1 skein apple green (leaves and inner symbol)
1 skein light leaf-green (veins and stems)

26 small pearl beads for Venus
24 blue and 24 green beads for jewels

Instructions

Tent stitch is used throughout, except for the following:-
1) Beads are sewn straight on to the canvas as a tent stitch using 6 strands of the same colour thread as the beads.
2) Optional blue border around the diamond as on Gemini.
See page 44 for chart.

To complete

There is an embroidered alphabet for Libra, see page 62 for chart.
The finished picture measures approximately 15 × 18cm (6 × 7in).

Seventh sign of the zodiac	Metal, copper
An air sign	Flowers, violet and grapevine
Positive	Plants, thyme and catmint
Cardinal	Flavour, warm
Ruling planet, Venus	Tree, ash
Motif, the scales	Day, Friday
Colours, pink, blue, pale green and leaf green	Number, 6
Gemstones, jade, emerald and blue opal	Keyword, balanced

Scorpio

23rd October to 22nd November
Scorpio is hard-working and serious minded
and will frequently follow a specialist profession, often medical.

Materials

Single canvas of 14 to 16 threads to 2.5cm (1in),
measuring 23 × 25cm (9 × 10½in)
Blunt-ended needle size 18
6-stranded mercerised cotton skeins in 11
colours, as follows:-
1 skein bright red (body)
1 skein cerise (legs, symbols and lettering)
1 skein charcoal grey (joints and eyes)
2 skeins white
3 skeins gold (background of diamond)
6 skeins dark turquoise (background)
1 skein bright turquoise (corners)
1 skein light turquoise (corners)
1 skein blue-green (carnation)

1 skein pale mauve (corners and carnation)
1 skein bright yellow (corners)

Instructions

Tent stitch is used throughout, except for the
following:-
1) The eyes can be worked with a charcoal grey
cross stitch
See page 48 for chart

To complete

There is a full alphabet for Scorpio, see page 64
for chart.
The finished picture measures approximately
13 × 15.5cm (5 × 6½in).

Eighth sign of the zodiac
A water sign
Negative
Fixed
Ruling planets, Mars and Pluto
Motif, the scorpion
Scorpio has two ruling planets
and three symbols:
second symbol – the eagle;
third symbol – the phoenix.
Colours, all hot reds, scarlet, blue,
green and lime yellow

Gemstones, ruby, bloodstone, topaz
and opal
Metals, iron and steel
Flowers, carnation and orchid
Plants, horseradish and sarsaparilla
Flavour, aromatic
Tree, blackthorn
Day, Tuesday
Number, 9
Keyword, desire

Sagittarius

23rd November to 22nd December
Sagittarius has great pride and discipline.
This sign uses great enthusiasm and inspiration for
self-expression and is often a writer or designer.

Materials

Single canvas of 14 to 16 threads to 2.5cm (1in), measuring 26.5 × 28cm (10½ × 11in)
Blunt-ended needle size 18
6-stranded mercerised cotton skeins in 10 colours, as follows:-
2 skeins white
2 skeins beige (background of diamond)
1 skein dark flesh
1 skein cerise (symbols and lettering)
1 skein wine (bow, horse's belly and features)
1 skein dark purple (inner legs and quiver)
1 skein purple (legs, tail, corners and lettering)
1 skein mauve (horse's back and corners)
1 skein lime green (clothes and corners)
4 skeins exactly (5 to be safe!) rich plum purple (background)

Instructions

Tent stitch is used throughout, except for the following:-
1) The strings of the bow which are worked in back stitch, in 2 strands of wine.
2) The arrow shaft is worked in back stitch (over the white tent stitch) in 6 strands of cerise.
3) The mouth is one back stitch in wine.
See page 50 for chart.

To complete

There is a full alphabet for Sagittarius showing a line where the colours change, see page 64 for chart.
The finished picture measures approximately 16.5 × 18cm (6½ × 7in).

Ninth sign of the zodiac	Metals, tin and pewter
A fire sign	Flowers, pinks and mimosa
Positive	Plant, dandelion
Mutable	Flavour, fragrant
Ruling planet, Jupiter	Tree, oak and lime
Motif, the archer is a centaur, which is half man, half horse	Day, Thursday
	Number, 3
Colours, purple, wine and deep blue	Keyword, voyager
Gemstones, topaz, sapphire and amethyst	

Capricorn

23rd December to 20th January
Capricorns are single-minded and patient at whatever
they are doing and also imaginative.
The influences of Uranus inspire this sign,
yet they can also have a tendency
to flit from project to project.

Materials

As the Capricorn colours are so dark, with no help from Saturn's black and the metal which is lead, it is necessary to turn to the gemstones for colour.

Single canvas of 14 to 16 threads to 2.5cm (1in), measuring 28 × 32cm (11 × 12½in)

Blunt-ended needle size 18

6-stranded mercerised cotton skeins in 14 colours, as follows:-

1 skein pale yellow (horns and hair)
1 skein gold (hair)
1 skein light brown (hair)
1 skein medium brown (hair)
1 skein red-brown (ears and beard)
3 skeins white
2 skeins jade (lettering, corners and tail)
1 skein indigo (horn shadows and features)
2 skeins dark blue (horns, tail, lettering and symbols)

1 skein delphinium blue (poppy)
3 skeins pinky mauve (background of diamond)
7 skeins dark pinky mauve (background)
1 skein dark turquoise (tail and corners)
1 skein bright turquoise (corners)

Instructions

Tent stitch is used throughout. See Page 54 for chart.

To complete

There is an embroidered alphabet for Capricorn, see page 62 for chart.

The finished picture measures approximately 18 × 21.5cm (7 × 8½in).

Tenth sign of the zodiac
An earth sign
Negative
Cardinal
Ruling planets, Saturn and Jupiter
Motif, the goat
Colours, charcoal, deep blue, black, white and navy
Gemstones, garnet, dark sapphire, jade, zircon, diamond and turquoise

Metal, lead
Flowers, poppy and hyacinth
Plants, comfrey root and thyme
Flavour, fresh
Tree, pine
Day, Saturday
Number, 8
Keyword, purpose

Aquarius

21st January to 19th February
Aquarius is creative in social ways, particularly in a
musical sphere and is of an idealistic nature.

Materials

Single canvas of 14 to 16 threads to 2.5cm (1in),
measuring 26.5 × 30.5cm (10½ × 12in)
Blunt-ended needle size 18
6-stranded mercerised cotton skeins in 15
colours, as follows:-
1 skein gold (background)
2 skeins light gold (background)
3 skeins yellow (background)
3 skeins white
1 skein dark blue-purple (lettering)
1 skein dark purple (carrier and water)
2 skeins purple (symbols and water)
1 skein bright mauve (cherries, carrier and
water)
1 skein royal blue (water)
1 skein delphinium blue (water)
2 skeins powder blue (symbol and water)
1 skein dark emerald (water)
1 skein dark turquoise (water and leaves)
1 skein bright turquoise (water)
1 skein soft blue-green (carrier and leaves)

Instructions

Tent stitch is used throughout, except for the
following:-
1) 6 bubbles over the water and 3 in the surf,
which are worked in cross stitch in various
colours.
See page 56 for chart.

To complete

There is no alphabet for Aquarius, but it is very
similar to Taurus. If any additional wording is
to be worked then the Scorpio alphabet would
be most suitable. See page 63 for chart.
The finished picture measures approximately
16.5 × 20.5 cm (6½ × 8in).

Eleventh sign of the zodiac
An air sign
Positive
Fixed
Ruling planets, Saturn and Uranus
Motif, the water carrier
Colours, purple, royal blue,
emerald and turquoise
Gemstones, garnet, emerald, sapphire,
jet and chalcedony

Metals, platinum, uranium and lead
Flowers, gentian and daffodil
Plants, valerian and snakeroot
Flavour, cool
Tree, cherry and peach
Day, Saturday
Number, 4
Keyword, intellect

Pisces

20th February to 20th March
Pisces is creative, a thinker, sensitive
and may also be psychic.

Materials

Single canvas of 14 to 16 threads to 2.5cm (1in),
measuring 23 × 25.5cm (9 × 10in)
Blunt-ended needle size 18
6-stranded mercerised cotton skeins in 10
colours, as follows:-
2 skeins white
1 skein yellow (sea, fish and corners)
1 skein lime (sea and fish)
1 skein sea-green (sea)
2 skeins mauve (sea and corners)
1 skein cerise (symbols and lettering)
1 skein royal blue (fish and corners)
1 skein dark emerald (fish and leaves)
1 skein bright green (fish and corners)
7 skeins dark blue (background)

Instructions

Tent stitch is used throughout, except for the
following:-
1) The fishes' eyes which are worked with a
French knot in royal blue in the centre of the 4
white tent stitches.
See page 60 for chart.

To complete

The alphabet for Scorpio can be used for Pisces
as they are the same, except for the 'C' and 'I',
see page 64 for chart. These letters can be taken
from the Pisces chart, see page 60.
The finished picture measures approximately
13.5 × 15cm (5¼ × 6in).

Twelfth sign of the zodiac
A water sign
Negative
Mutable
Ruling planets, Neptune and Jupiter
Motif, the fishes
Colours, soft sea-green, violet and blue
Gemstones, amethyst, aquamarine,
pearl and opal

Metal, platinum
Flowers, water lily and tulip
Plant, yarrow
Flavour, enticing
Tree, willow
Day, Thursday
Number, 7
Keyword, psychic

Lettering for zodiac embroideries

The lettering and numbers can be used for additional information, such as names and birthdates, noting that the number '1' is simply a vertical line. The canvas will need to be increased in size and yarn allowed for any extra wording.

Embroidered lettering for Cancer (top), Capricorn (middle), Libra (bottom), also numbering (top).

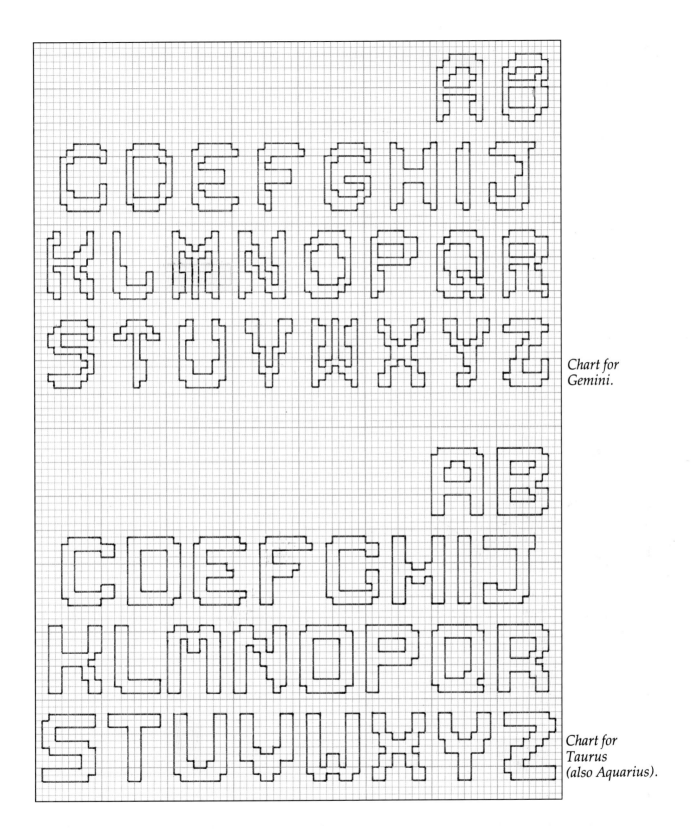

Chart for Gemini.

Chart for Taurus (also Aquarius).

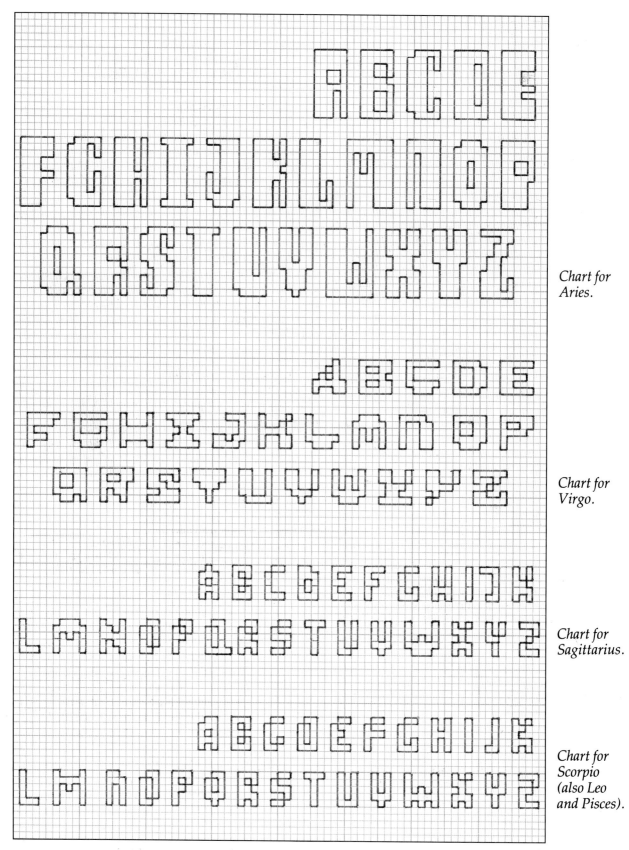

Chart for Aries.

Chart for Virgo.

Chart for Sagittarius.

Chart for Scorpio (also Leo and Pisces).